The Thread of Life

The Thread of Life

Heather Masco

Foreword by Vicki Proffit

RESOURCE *Publications* · Eugene, Oregon

THE THREAD OF LIFE

Copyright © 2021 Heather Masco. All rights reserved. Except for brief quotations in critical publications or reviews, no part of this book may be reproduced in any manner without prior written permission from the publisher. Write: Permissions, Wipf and Stock Publishers, 199 W. 8th Ave., Suite 3, Eugene, OR 97401.

Resource Publications
An Imprint of Wipf and Stock Publishers
199 W. 8th Ave., Suite 3
Eugene, OR 97401

www.wipfandstock.com

PAPERBACK ISBN: 978-1-6667-1505-7
HARDCOVER ISBN: 978-1-6667-1506-4
EBOOK ISBN: 978-1-6667-1507-1

SEPTEMBER 7, 2021

This book is dedicated

to those affected by childhood sexual abuse

and sex trafficking—

may this story provide you with light

in your time of darkness;

to my parents, who love me unconditionally,

and to my husband,

who inspires me

to be the best version of myself—

may this story fill you with peace.

Contents

Foreword by Vicki Proffit — xi

Preface — xiii

Acknowledgements — xv

Warning — xvii

~ Fear ~ — 1
  Bible Verses for "Fear" — 12

~ Faith ~ — 13
  Bible Verses for "Faith" — 26

~ Forgiveness ~ — 27
  Bible Verses for "Forgiveness" — 42

~ Hope ~ — 43
  Bible Verses for "Hope" — 54

Epilogue — 55

Resources — 57

Sarah's Home — 59

Information on Human Trafficking — 61

Permissions

Sarah's Home. "Information on Human Trafficking." In *The New Donor Packet*. Used by permission of Vicki Proffit, Executive Director of Sarah's Home on 04/07/2021. All rights reserved.

Scriptures marked ESV are taken from the THE HOLY BIBLE, ENGLISH STANDARD VERSION (ESV): Scriptures taken from THE HOLY BIBLE, ENGLISH STANDARD VERSION ® Copyright© 2001 by Crossway, a publishing ministry of Good News Publishers. Used by permission.

Scriptures marked KJV are taken from the KING JAMES VERSION (KJV): KING JAMES VERSION, public domain.

Scripture quotations marked (NIV) are taken from the Holy Bible, New International Version®, NIV®. Copyright © 1973, 1978, 1984, 2011 by Biblica, Inc.® Used by permission of Zondervan. All rights reserved worldwide. www.zondervan.com The "NIV" and "New International Version" are trademarks registered in the United States Patent and Trademark Office by Biblica, Inc.®

Scriptures marked NKJV are taken from the NEW KING JAMES VERSION (NKJV): Scripture taken from the NEW

Permissions

KING JAMES VERSION®. Copyright© 1982 by Thomas Nelson, Inc. Used by permission. All rights reserved.

Scripture quotations marked (NLT) are taken from the Holy Bible, New Living Translation, copyright © 1996, 2004, 2007, 2013, 2015 by Tyndale House Foundation. Used by permission of Tyndale House Publishers, Inc., Carol Stream, Illinois 60188. All rights reserved.

Scriptures marked WEB are taken from the THE WORLD ENGLISH BIBLE (WEB): WORLD ENGLISH BIBLE, public domain.

Foreword

By Vicki Proffit
Executive Director of Sarah's Home

My heart is attuned to the silent scream of far too many in our world: I am broken! I am worthless! I have no hope!

As a foster parent, as the founding director of Teen Challenge House of Promise, a home for broken women and their children, and now Executive Director of Sarah's Home, a home for rescued sex trafficked teen girls, that scream is heart wrenching to me ... so much so, that I had difficulty reading *The Thread of Life*. But this is a must read! Countless people have experienced this horrible, wrenching trauma and are crying for help. Each of us either need the help or can be equipped to have compassion to help others that are dear to us.

In my experience, I have come to know that Jesus Christ is the only hope, the only answer, the only One who can see the oozing wounds and heal every layer from within each of us.

Foreword

I have heard the story embedded in *The Thread of Life* far too many times. A survivor can walk closely beside others who are struggling to find their way out of the darkness to light: out of their night terrors, out of their worthlessness, out of their shame because the survivor has already done so and has found healing. Heather Masco does this in this story with great insight.

I am so excited to introduce this treasure to the precious victims at Sarah's Home. But I am just as excited for the millions of other victims in our world to read this story over and over as they walk out of fear into faith, through forgiveness into hope, becoming survivors instead of victims.

Maybe you have never experienced this secret pain, but I believe that if you ask the Healer, Jesus Christ, he will show you someone to share this life giving story with who needs it.

Preface

THERE IS A DARK REALITY that exists within our world that we do not like to discuss or want to think about; but we must. We must find a way to bring the issue of child rape, pornography, and molestation to the forefront of our minds so that it can be eradicated. There are many children currently being molested and raped behind the closed doors of their homes, schools, churches, and within their neighborhoods. Some choose to run away and find themselves in worse situations; while others are kidnapped, sold as slaves into the sex trade, and forced to perform the unthinkable. It is a dark world for these children. They need rescuing. They need their stories to be told and their realities to be believed. They need understanding, compassion, and love. They need to heal. Healing, for these individuals, can only come through the grace of Jesus Christ. Only he can mend their broken hearts, their wounded bodies, and their scarred souls. This poem is for them. I pray for them to be rescued from their devastating circumstances and for emotional, physical, and spiritual healing through Jesus Christ to take place for each and everyone of them. My heart aches and hopes for them.

Acknowledgements

FIRST AND FOREMOST, I would like to thank my husband, Roger, for listening to and critiquing the various stages of this book. He offered me continuous support throughout the process, kept me moving forward when hurdles and difficulties arose, and walked with me throughout this journey. I am also grateful to my parents who taught me to believe in myself, to dream big, and to trust in Jesus. A special thanks also goes out to Kaleb for pushing me to reach for the stars and challenging me grow as a writer, and to Sam for being a light to me in moments of darkness.

Furthermore, I would like to thank Colleen Stokes, Laura McKinley, Jennifer Minerly, Elizabeth Zasowski, Lisa Deal, Cindy Perry, Alexis Jorgensen, and Alison Barnes for their input and assistance as I worked on preparing the final manuscript. I also want to thank Vicki Proffit for believing in this book in its early stages.

Finally, I thank my Lord and Savior, Jesus Christ, for the gift of salvation, unconditional love, hope, and eternity.

To any other individuals that I have not listed here, but should have, and all those that I have listed, thank you again. I am so grateful to each and everyone of you.

Warning

This book contains graphic language about rape and may trigger flashbacks or strong emotional responses for some individuals.

~ Fear ~

"And I am convinced that nothing can ever separate us from God's love. Neither death nor life, neither angels nor demons, neither our fears for today nor our worries about tomorrow—not even the powers of hell can separate us from God's love."

—Romans 8:38–39, NLT

I lie in fear.
Waiting.
Knowing.
Preparing myself
for the agony
that awaits me.
I wish I could hide—
or disappear—
or simply vanish.
But I'm stuck,
here.
My lot.
My hell.
"God,
why me?
Help me!
Save me
from this monster!
Please, God—
just take me away."

I hear the thud
of feet
in the hallway
moving towards
my room.
The old floor groans
under his weight,
echoing the despair
of my heavy heart.
I wish he wouldn't come;
that he would just

forget about me
and leave me
alone.
I have nothing to offer him.
I'm just a girl,
not even a teenager.
Why should he want me?
WHY ME?

But I know—
even as I hear
the cursed cry
of the aged wood,
that he has not
forgotten me.
So,
I try
to prepare myself.
What else can I do?
I can't fight.
It does no good.
I'd end up in worse shape
than if I just give him
what he wants—
me.

Anyway,
it doesn't matter.
No one else
is home.
My stupid mom.
How can she not know

what he is doing to me?
Is she blind?
Or does she just not care?
I won't fight.
I'll just—
just pretend I'm asleep.
I won't look at him.
Or help him.
Perhaps if I act dead,
he'll get bored
and go away.

I hear metal slide
like knives
against themselves,
as he turns the doorknob.
I slow my breathing.
Hopefully,
he can't hear my heart
stampeding
against my chest.
I feel the mattress
sag towards him
as he sits beside me,
and I wish—
I were dead.
Inside
my imprisoned body,
I'm screaming
and shouting
as loud as I can,
"GO AWAY!

LEAVE ME ALONE!
DON'T TOUCH ME!"
But no one hears.
No one cares.
I'm all alone—
just me
and him.

He is supposed to protect me
—to care about me.
So how can he do this to me?
He brushes the hair
from my face.
I inhale slowly,
exhale silently.
I keep my eyes relaxed
—closed.
Lifeless,
except for the rise
and fall of my chest
with each breath.
If I could just—
force myself
to stop breathing—
I would.

He rolls me onto my back
like a rag doll—I flop over:
limp,
like my spirit.
He pushes
the blankets aside.

Pulls up my night gown.
The freezing night air
bites my exposed skin,
making me shudder.
I do not move.
He yanks off my underwear
and forces my legs
apart with his knees,
then pins me
against the bed—
once my refuge,
now my place
of torture.

I hold my breath.
My eyes clench shut,
as red, searing pain
slices through my body,
stabbing me with each thrust.
A single whimper
slides from my lips,
even as I swallow down
the screams
that try to escape
my mouth.
Voiceless tears
seep
from the edges
of my eyes.
I hold my breath
—against the pain.
I hold my breath

—against this life.

My lungs begin to burn
—on fire,
building
with intensity.
My heart weeps.
My soul cries out
to God.
I force myself
to ignore the pain,
to ignore this beast
as he destroys
—my innocence
—my childhood
and unravels
—my trust
—myself.
My lungs,
consumed in flames,
hurt less
than life,
but distract
me
from this
bestial
moment.

Sweet
nothingness
begins shading
the fringes

of my mind,
fading reality
—
taking over
my thoughts,

until
I

fade

away.

Bible Verses for "Fear"

"Don't be afraid, for I am with you. Don't be discouraged, for I am your God. I will strengthen you and help you. I will hold you up with my victorious right hand" (Isaiah 41:10, NLT).

"Jesus told him, 'Don't be afraid; just believe'" (Mark 5:36, NIV).

"Say to those with fearful hearts, 'Be strong, do not fear; your God will come, . . .'" (Isaiah 35:4, NLT).

"He will cover you with his feathers. Under his wings you will find refuge. His faithfulness is a shield and rampart. You shall not be afraid of the terror by night, nor of the arrow that flies by day; . . ." (Psalm 91:4–5, WEB).

"But the Lord is faithful, and he will strengthen you and protect you from the evil one" (2 Thessalonians 3:3, NIV).

"Do not be afraid of them; the Lord your God himself will fight for you" (Deuteronomy 3:22, NIV).

"The Lord will rescue me from every evil attack and will bring me safely to his heavenly kingdom. To him be glory forever and ever. Amen" (2 Timothy 4:18, NIV).

~ Faith ~

"In all circumstances take up the shield of faith, with which you can extinguish all the flaming darts of the evil one; and take the helmet of salvation and the sword of the Spirit, which is the Word of God, . . ."

—Ephesians 6:16–17, ESV

Years later,
I sit before
a counselor
yearning to restitch
the tattered fabric
of my soul;
to mend my feelings
of being helpless,
powerless,
and voiceless;
to gather
together the
stained rags of
my past
into material
worth salvaging.
It is time
to repair
myself.

This is the session,
the moment
we've worked toward.
She will lead me through
the insidious tunnels
of my memory,
where a monster
stalks me;
lurking;
waiting to finish me;
to tear the remains
of my sanity

to shreds.
I'm scared.
I'm not sure,
if I—
if I'm strong
enough.
Or that
I'm actually
ready.
But,
I have to try,
and—
I'm not alone.
Jesus,
my Savior,
will go before me.
I need only to
trust.

Funny,
how one little word
can be so powerful
—to trust anyone,
requires
vulnerability,
faith,
courage.
Those traits
are kinked threads
sticking out haphazardly
from the torn remnants
of my heart.

Broken.
Frayed.
But they remain
attached;
so with them,
I will start.

We pray,
"Dear Lord,
please lead us
through the
nightmares of my past.
Help me know that
you are with me;
that you were
always with me;
that I was
never
alone.
Help me
to trust you,
to rely on you.
Please mend
my torn
and weary
soul.
Amen."
And so,
we begin.

I'm back in my bed.
Waiting.

Listening for the groan
of the floor
and the twisting metal
of the handle.
My heart drums
against my chest.
Sweat beads across
my body,
pooling down my back.
I'm burning on fire—

"Mary! Mary!
Breathe!
You are not alone.
You are safe.
Focus.
Focus on my voice.
This is a memory.
He cannot hurt you."

I let go
of the scorching air
trapped
inside my chest.
Slowly,
I unclench
my jaw
and relax
my fisted
hands.

"Now, Mary,

I want you to
feel God's presence.
Imagine Jesus
wrapping
his protective arms
around you.
Feel the warmth
of his love
encircling you.
Soothing your fears.
Jesus will not
let you go.
Let's continue."

Evil enters my room.
Sits on my bed.
Brushes the hair
away from my face.
Rolls me over.
I freeze.
Motionless.
Mute.
A mannequin.

"Mary,
know that God
is with you.
Focus on his
calming peace.
Evil cannot
harm you."

I exhale.
Air rushes out,
of my tired lungs.
I concentrate
on feeling Jesus's
presence
and knowing—
I'm not alone.

"Mary, I want you
to visualize
a bright light.
This light illuminates
the darkness.
Shadows
cannot penetrate it.
This is the light
of Jesus.
It radiates
love,
peace,
hope.
As you feel
Jesus holding you,
I want you to see
his light
encompassing
your body;
separating you
from evil.
Allow Jesus,
to be your buffer.

*Allow him—
to be penetrated.
He can take your pain
away. Let him
carry this burden
for you."*

I close my eyes.
I'm in my room.
The monster
is pinning me
to my bed.
I force myself to
visualize
the bright light
of Jesus
shielding
my fragile,
limp body.

The monster
rams himself
against the light;
but I feel
—I feel—
only warmth
and peace.
I am not alone.
Jesus cloaks
my spirit,
shielding
my soul.

Evil cannot
touch me.
The shackles
of fear,
of being
voiceless,
and powerless,
holding me
captive—
open;
releasing me.
I feel as though,
I'm floating,
feather light
and free.
The shades
of darkness
clinging
to the fringes
of my
scarred mind,
fade away.

But I
remain.
Alert.
Breathing in
the sweet breath
of Jesus Christ.
While the thread
of life,
of love,

of trust,
and faith—
begins sewing
together
the frayed tatters
of my heart
and mind;
restitching
my memories
to reflect
the healing
presence
of Jesus Christ,
my Lord
and Savior.

Bible Verses for "Faith"

"And whatever you ask in prayer, you will receive, if you have faith" (Matthew 21:22, ESV).

"Trust in the Lord with all your heart; do not depend on your own understanding. Seek his will in all you do, and he will show you which path to take" (Proverbs 3:5–6, ESV).

"And the peace of God, which transcends all understanding, will guard your hearts and minds in Christ Jesus" (Philippians 4:7, NIV).

"The Lord says, 'I will rescue those who love me. I will protect those who trust in my name. When they call on me, I will answer; I will be with them in trouble. I will rescue and honor them. I will reward them with a long life and give them my salvation'" (Psalm 91:14–16, NLT).

"Then your light will break forth like the dawn, and your healing will quickly appear; then your righteousness will go before you, and the glory of the Lord will be your rear guard" (Isaiah 58:8, NIV).

"The light shines in the darkness, and the darkness has not overcome it" (John 1:5, NIV).

"The Lord is my light and my salvation; whom shall I fear? The Lord is the strength of my life; of whom shall I be afraid?" (Psalm 27:1, KJV).

~ Forgiveness ~

"I am the true vine, and my Father is the gardener. He cuts off every branch in me that bears no fruit, while every branch that does bear fruit he prunes so that it will be even more fruitful. You are already clean because of the word that I have spoken to you. Remain in me, as I also remain in you. No branch can bear fruit by itself; it must remain in the vine. Neither can you bear fruit unless you remain in me. I am the vine; you are the branches. If you remain in me and I in you, you will bear much fruit; apart from me you can do nothing."

—John 15:1–7, NIV

As the warm reds
and browns of
autumn fade
into the glittering
white of winter,
nourishing the soil
for the green
birth of spring—
Jesus mended,
cut, stitched,
and gathered
my torn spirit
into the makings
of a beautiful
masterpiece.
I started
letting go of
my embedded fears
and suffocating
anxieties;
while I worked to
repair my shredded
confidence
in others.

God washed away
the grime of my sins
and self doubt,
allowing
the vibrant
red of his love,
the brilliant blue

of faith and trust,
and the rich green
of new beginnings
to shine brightly
within my life.
Slowly—
ever so gently,
Jesus peeled away
the protective layers
I'd built around
my heart and mind,
loosening their
restrictive tethers;
until he
uncovered a
blackened,
layer of decay.

"Jesus, what is this?"
I asked;
confused,
worried.

*"This is your
hatred.
Hatred towards
your perpetrator,
your mother,
yourself."*

Appalled—
I turned away.

"How do I fix this?"

*"You must learn
to forgive—
you must shear
the hatred
from your life."*

"But, God,
I can't
forgive them—
they deserve
my vengeance.
It's my right to hate
what defiled me
and allowed me
to be defiled."

*"Mary,
you deserve
to live
your life
free from evil
and from this
rot decaying
your soul.
You deserve
to live in
my peace
and in the
comfort of
my undying love.*

*You believed in me;
asked for
forgiveness—
and I forgave you.
But you must
now learn
how to forgive
for yourself."*

"I can't do
what you're
asking of me,
God," I cried!

Frustrated,
and troubled—
I ran.
I ran from
Jesus.
I ran as far
as my legs
would take me.
I ran for
my lost
innocence.
I ran for
the little girl
whose childhood
was stripped
from her.
I ran to
ease the pain

—to drown out
what Jesus
was asking of me.
How could I
forgive that bastard?
He was evil.
I hated him.
No way—
could I
forgive him.

And my mother—
she didn't stop him.
She ignored
the signs
and instead,
turned a blind eye
to my pain,
choosing him
over me.
She let me down—
crushing
my hope.

And me,
what did I do
to stop the rape?
I fought—
but
gave up.
I should have
kept fighting.

I should have
yelled
and screamed.
I should have
run away.
I should have
told someone,
anyone,
somehow,
someway—
but I didn't.
I became a
mannequin.
I didn't
deserve
forgiveness.
I didn't
deserve
love.

Sobbing,
I stumbled—
blinded by tears.
My knees
crumbled
and I
sunk to
the ground.
Bitterness swelled
inside me;
mixing with anger
until they bubbled

over and
poured
from my eyes.
How dare Jesus
ask me to forgive—
when the world
told me,
I should hate.

But if—
if hate was
the answer—
then why was
my spirit rotting
from the
inside out?
Why was it
separating me
from Jesus?
"WHY JESUS?
WHY IS THIS
HAPPENING?"
I screamed!

"Hate is fed
to you
by the devil.
It is evil.
It invades
your soul,
like vines
that wrap

*around
your heart,
and mind;
strangling them;
turning them black;
consuming
your spirit;
filling you
with darkness."*

"Lord, I
don't want
to be filled
with hate,
but I'm not
ready—or
strong enough
to forgive."

*"Dear child,
I do not expect
you to forgive
on your own.
I am with you
—always.
I will give you
the strength.
Just ask me
to help you—
and I will."*

A waterfall

of tears
rushed
from my eyes.
My heart
pounded
against my chest;
shaking,
I bowed my head.
In a faint whisper
I prayed,
"Dear Lord,
help me.
Help me learn
to forgive—
my mom."
Sobbing,
I continued—
"Help me let go
of the hatred
and bitterness
I feel towards
my assailant.
Help
me—
to forgive
him.
And Lord,
my God—
help me
learn
to forgive
myself."

As I prayed,
—distraught,
—humbled,
I envisioned myself
cutting away the
blackened,
decaying fabric
adhered
to my soul.
Jesus's light,
his power,
ignited the scissors
in fire
as he wrapped
his hand around mine
and together—
we sheared
and cauterized
the hate,
the evil
from
my heart
and mind.

As we mended
my spirit,
forgiveness
seeped into the
vacated space,
filling the void;
while a heaviness,

I never knew
existed,
lifted from me.
I felt—
weightless,
riding
on a cloud
of peace;
while
a joyful stillness
rose within me,
—and
something
else—
a feeling of
anticipation,
of expectation
that God's
promises
would be kept;
that he was faithful;
that he would provide.
Stunned by this
metamorphosis
within myself,
I paused—
realizing
that I'd been
enfolded
into the
fibers of
hope.

Bible Verses for "Forgiveness"

"But anyone who hates a brother or sister is in the darkness and walks around in the darkness. They do not know where they are going, because the darkness has blinded them" (1 John 2:11, NIV).

"Get rid of all bitterness, rage, anger, harsh words, and slander, as well as all types of evil behavior. Instead, be kind to each other, tenderhearted, forgiving one another, just as God through Christ has forgiven you" (Ephesians 4:31–32, NLT).

"because, if you confess with your mouth that Jesus is Lord and believe in your heart that God raised him from the dead, you will be saved. For with the heart one believes and is justified, and with the mouth one confesses and is saved" (Romans 10:9–10, ESV).

"so that your faith might not rest in the wisdom of men but in the power of God" (1 Corinthians 2:5, ESV).

"Do not be overcome by evil, but overcome evil with good" (Romans 12:21, NIV).

"I can do all things through Christ who strengthens me" (Philippians 4:13, NKJV).

"For once you were full of darkness, but now you have the light from the Lord. So live as people of light! For this light within you produces only what is good, right and true" (Ephesians 5:8–9, NLT).

~ Hope ~

"There is a time for everything and a season for every activity under the heavens: a time to be born and a time to die, a time to plant and a time to uproot, a time to kill and a time to heal, a time to tear down and a time to build, a time to weep and a time to laugh, a time to mourn and a time to dance, a time to scatter stones and a time to gather them, a time to embrace and a time to refrain from embracing, a time to search and a time to give up, a time to keep and a time to throw away, a time to tear and a time to mend, a time to be silent and a time to speak, a time to love and a time to hate, a time for war and time for peace ... [God] has made everything beautiful in its time. He has also set eternity in the human heart; ... "

—Ecclesiastes 3:1–8, 11, NIV

I am Mary—
a survivor
of rape.

For years,
I let the
fleeting,
momentary
pleasures of a
feeble man
imprison me—
tethering me
to his evil sins
and the
nightmares of
my past.
That is,
until Jesus
rescued me
from my self-pity,
from my shame,
and
from my fear.

He delicately
began sewing
together the
torn and frayed
edges of my soul.
He helped me
face my
monster—

trimming
the fear
from my mind;
blunting the
blade of evil
memories;
shielding me
from the harsh
contours
of my dreams.
He filled the
darkness with
magnificent light;
shriveling the
suffocating vines
of hatred,
making them
—feasible,
—manageable
for me
to cut loose;
to sear them
from my life;
allowing
forgiveness
to sooth my
scars
and heal
my tattered
spirit.

Jesus helped

me sew
and patch
myself—
my world—
into a
vibrant tapestry;
pieced together
with
roughened edges,
repaired holes,
torn seams,
snags,
and rags,
creating a
masterpiece
of beauty—
resonating
his love
for me.

He sewed
my faith
in him
into the fabric
of my being;
instilling me—
with the
assurance of
his promises;
rooted
in his
Word;

stitching me
together
with the
thread of life—
hope.

I am
guaranteed—
peace
that transcends
all understanding,
never ending
love,
abounding joy,
and blessings;
along with
the security
and knowledge
that I am
not alone,
and
that I am
promised
eternal life
in heaven
with
my Lord
and Savior.

I am—
now
an intricate

patchwork
quilt—
wondrously
comforting
and
compassionate;
portraying the
varied hues
of emotion,
the irregularities
of experience,
the woven
strength
of
perseverance,
and the
limitless
power
of God's
love.

I am—
sewn
together
by hope,
the
silken
thread
of
life.

I am—

a
warrior
who
conquered
evil
with the
sword
of
Jesus Christ.

I am—
a
survivor
of
rape.

I am—
a
child
of
God.

I
am—
fearless.

I
am—
forgiven.

I
am—

loved.

I—

am
Mary

.

Bible Verses for "Hope"

"For everyone who has been born of God overcomes the world. And this is the victory that has overcome the world—our faith" (1 John 5:4, ESV).

"I have been crucified with Christ. It is no longer I who live, but Christ who lives in me. And the life I now live in the flesh I live by faith in the Son of God, who loved me and gave himself for me" (Galatians 2:20, ESV).

"Now faith is the assurance of things hoped for, the conviction of things not seen" (Hebrews 11:1, ESV).

"Not only that, but we rejoice in our sufferings, knowing that suffering produces endurance, and endurance produces character, and character produces hope, and hope does not put us to shame, because God's love has been poured into our hearts through the Holy Spirit who has been given to us" (Romans 5:3–5, ESV).

"For I know the plans I have for you, declares the Lord, 'Plans to prosper you and not to harm you. Plans to give you hope and a future'" (Jeremiah 29:11, NIV).

"But those who hope in the Lord will renew their strength. They will soar on wings like eagles; they will run and not grow weary, they will walk and not faint" (Isaiah 40:31, NIV).

"May the God of hope fill you with all joy and peace as you trust in him, so that you may overflow with hope by the power of the Holy Spirit" (Romans 15:13, NIV).

Epilogue

"The Lord is my shepherd;
I shall not want.
He makes me lie down in green pastures.
He leads me beside still waters.
He restores my soul.
He leads me in paths of righteousness
for his name's sake.

~Fear~
Even though I walk through the valley
of the shadow of death,

~Faith~
I will fear no evil,
for you are with me;
your rod and your staff,
they comfort me.

~Forgiveness~
You prepare a table before me
in the presence of my enemies;
you anoint my head with oil;
my cup overflows.

~Hope~
Surely goodness and mercy shall follow me
all the days of my life,
and I shall dwell in the house of the Lord
forever."

—Psalm 23:1–6, ESV

Resources

If you or someone you love is being sexually abused or has been abused and needs help or support, please call:

1.800.656.HOPE (4673)

or use the live chat app at:

rainn.org

(Rape, Abuse & Incest National Network)
There are many resources available through this website.

You can also find hotlines and resources at:

www.acf.hhs.gov

(Administration for Children and Families)

Resources

Victims and survivors of human trafficking can also find support and resources by calling:

The National Human Trafficking Hotline:

> *1-888-373-7888 (TTY 711)*
> *or*
> *Text: 233733*

or visiting their website:

> *humantraffickinghotline.org*

If you or a loved one is in immediate danger, please call:
911

Sarah's Home[1]

SARAH'S HOME IS A RESIDENTIAL PROGRAM located in Colorado for girls ages 12 up to 18 who have been rescued from sex trafficking. This program offers these victimized teens a safe, faith-based haven where they can find physical, emotional, and spiritual healing. Residents of this program receive medical care, counseling, therapy, spiritual guidance, skills training for life, jobs, and relationships. In addition, each girl is provided with an Individualized Education Plan (IEP) through Aspire Academy, an accredited private school established solely for the residents of Sarah's Home. Through Aspire Academy, these girls are able to recover high school credits, work towards receiving their high school diploma, while also learning how to set both life and career goals.

The concept for Sarah's Home was developed after the Rocky Mountain District Women's ministries realized that there are an estimated 300,000 minors being sexually trafficked annually right here within the United States, with less then 1 percent of those who are rescued finding placement within residential treatment programs, simply because so few programs exist for these victims. Of the programs that do exist, few are Christ centered. Thus, Sarah's Home was

---

1. Sarah's Home. *New Donor Packet.*

born into existence in 2013 and has since been successfully helping rescued teen girls find healing.

In addition, Sarah's Home Corporation recently identified that there are few residential treatment programs with in the United States for teen boys who have also been rescued from sex trafficking. As a result, this corporation is now working to develop a sustainable home, similar to Sarah's Home, especially for them. Please note that Sarah's Home and its corporation receive no government funding. They rely solely on funds donated to the organization from individuals and companies whose hearts are tender towards these victimized children and who have been inspired by Jesus to give financially to them to support their mission. In an effort to help fund the miraculous resource this organization is providing to rescued teens of sex trafficking, a significant portion of the profits earned by the author from the sale of this book will be donated to Sarah's Home and its corporation. To learn more about Sarah's Home or to find more ways to support their mission, please visit their website at www.SarahsHome.us or email them at info@sarahshome.us. You may also call them at (719) 347-3026.

Information on Human Trafficking[2]

What is Human Trafficking?

Simply put, human trafficking is modern-day slavery through force, fraud, or coercion. It also includes any commercial sex act, if the person is under 18 years of age, regardless of whether any form of coercion is involved. Sex trafficking is the fastest-growing business of organized crime and the third-largest criminal enterprise in the world.

Is human trafficking really happening in the United States?

People often think human trafficking only happens in other countries, but human trafficking is happening right here in America, with American children. As of October 2017, the FBI has recovered more than 6,500 children that were victims of sex trafficking. Trafficking occurs all over the United States – truck stops, suburban neighborhoods, strip clubs, big cities, schools, churches, and small towns. Cell phones and the internet have made it convenient to sell underage girls for sex, and you can order girls almost as easily as ordering a pizza.

---

2. Sarah's Home. "Information on Human Trafficking."

RESOURCES

Who are the trafficking victims?

There are several ways that girls and boys can become trafficked in the U.S. A friend, boyfriend, family member, or a complete stranger will trick, threaten or coerce her into the commercial sex trade. In rare cases, she will be kidnapped. The most vulnerable victims are those who come from abusive homes where a girl has been abused, molested, raped, or neglected to the point that she cannot stay at home. It has been estimated that within 48 hours of leaving home 1 out of 3 runaways will be approached by a trafficker or pimp. These runaway girls are extremely vulnerable because they are typically desperate and are willing to accept the care of a stranger in exchange for sex.

www.ingramcontent.com/pod-product-compliance
Lightning Source LLC
Chambersburg PA
CBHW071740040426
42446CB00012B/2414